GW01458163

The Artificial Parisienne

Sue Burge is a freelance creative writing and film-studies tutor, mentor and editor. She is based in North Norfolk, UK. Her poems have appeared in a wide range of journals and in themed anthologies on science fiction, modern Gothic, illness, Britishness, endangered birds, WWI and the pandemic. Sue's first collection, *In the Kingdom of Shadows* (Live Canon), and debut pamphlet, *Lumière* (Hedgehog Poetry Press), were both published in 2018. Her second pamphlet, *The Saltwater Diaries* (Hedgehog Poetry Press), was published in 2020, followed by her second collection, *Confetti Dancers* (Live Canon), in 2021.

To Lee,
Hope you enjoy this
taste of Paris!

warmest wishes,
Sue
London, Jan' 24

First Published in 2024

by Live Canon Poetry Ltd
www.livecanon.co.uk

978-1-909703-56-8

A CIP catalogue record for this book is available from the British Library.

to my other self, whoever she may have become

Contents

A reverse abecedarian in praise of Paris   7

Snapshots   8

She is an erratic   11

La Goutte d'Or   12

Zuihitsu: the year of the thief   13

Mon Cher Lucien   18

Marché aux Puces, Porte de Vanves   19

The Paris Project — Cento I   20

Où est le Métro s'il-vous-plait?   21

Paris is a blonde   23

I find a photo of my imaginary parents in the Paris flea-market   24

Discovering Calentica (1986)   25

Paris is a Palimpsest   26

Cinematic   27

Mapping It   28

Reincarnation as the Eiffel Tower   29

A Thanksgiving Dinner as described in *The Alice B Toklas Cookbook*   30

Excavation   31

The Artificial Parisienne   32

She is the woman I should have been   34

Le Petit Prince   35

This is where   36

I am building Paris in my bedroom   37

Bagatelle   38

In Which A Middle-Aged Woman in Primark
Jeans Denies Her Invisibility   40

The Paris Project — Cento II   41

Apprenticeship   42

In Printemps Department Store   43

The Distant Place   44

La Charlotte de l'Ile   45

Flâneuse   46

The Cemeteries of Paris   47

Headstones   49

The Animal Cemetery Calls Her Name   52

This Place   54

Balade of the Fallen   55
Barbès Rochechouart   56
The Paris Project — Cento III   57
Versailles — Spring, Winter   58
A postcard from the ex   59
Paris is a paint-chart   60
La Reine   61
Les Jardins du Ruisseau, Paris 18ème   62
The Bees of Paris   64

Acknowledgments   65

another me speeding through the air, another me waving
from a train window watching you
waving from a train window watching me.

From 'Sometimes I think My Body Leaves a Shape in the Air'
(*The Carrying* by Ada Limón — Corsair Poetry 2018)

A reverse abecedarian in praise of Paris

this city is a jazz riff high as a skylark shouting *yes yes yes* to
April   this city is an expletive on the webby wad of your
tongue   it is not a valentine's card or a passive verb   this
city is a crucible for umbrellas   a tender prism   a slow
dance with no stoplights   this city is retrofitted with
cobbles and revolutionary baguettes   this city is
acquisitive and pronounceable   a psycho-geographic love
letter   this city is overused   a never-ending mosquito bite
saying *look at my lovely toys all spire and steeple and dome*   this
city thinks it's a kingdom   will make a jumble sale of your
heart   is an implausible impetuous impinger of your
dreams   this city is held in the hands of saints   an
unshareable galette des rois   it's a fickle flirty madame
blowing lipstick in your eyes   this city is a raised eyebrow
a dust-bath for little sparrows and all their bright chansons
this city will never be a cardigan   it's a bourrée executed
when the Seine runs red with sunset   this city is an abyss
and I'm still falling because this city is

Snapshots

i. Winterborn 1961 — no photograph available

I like to think I emerged
to a sultry New Wave soundtrack —
that the drizzle of Surbiton
was not enough to welcome me,
for I was, briefly, welcome,
with my pulsing fontanelle
and hungry eyes, blue with knowledge.
I can't open the tight-bound book
of that day but it's true
my first word was *Liberté,*
& the first thing I held in my fist
was not finger or rattle
but firework.

ii. In cheap Kodak — A café on the Champs Elysées circa 1978

I unroll the mythology of me

remember the self-conscious tilt
of my empty cup

how every head seemed to turn away
to unsee my too-long skirt

my hand-me-down shirt;
I can't remember how we lost each other

but here you are
corrupted with a wash of pink

an unwanted Hollywood sunset
        unwinding

iii. Paris 1979: snapshot without a camera

This is how it was that night
        the lights strung across the boulevard
your face wolverine in the fluorescence
        we improvised jazz riffs on the métro

Now each stop feels everyday, silent,
        your face faltering on my retina

iv. Paris, 1980: In the dark, with no flash

Where did you lose it?
Somewhere in Northern Paris, 1980
in a chambre de bonne
shared chiotte in the hallway
shower over the sink

after a soirée
cheap wine   pain complet
supermarché camembert

a nudging blunt-nosed seeking
an invited rupture
there should be a blue plaque
over the doorway
of this unfindable building

v. Paris, early 80s: taken with an Argentinian lens

Hector and Maria from Argentina
an encounter at Père Lachaise in winter sunlight —
their letters arrive opened, thumbed
they send her a copy of Borges' *Labyrinths*
she wonders if this is code
at night she flyposts Paris with her anarchist comrades
they blame her for the hunger strikes
want to ransom her
Une Anglaise pour Bobby Sands!

vi. Paris 1999, crane shot

She wants to sculpt the millennium
       using the dust from the statues
of a thousand fallen dictators.
       She shapes the paste
into an icon of the future;
       I hear it's one of the few things
you can see from space;
       the Great Wall of China,
the lights of Paris, her face.

chambre de bonne: literally "maid's room" — closest English equivalent "bedsit"
chiotte: crude slang for "toilet"

She is an erratic

                          in a city of limestone
a stray, yearning to be named.

She worships the golden boy
on the Bastille column

end-stopped with stars
a gilded tiptoe away from flight.

His gossip is true and excellent
as rising sap. He understands

why Napoleon's symbol is a bee
knows a wren who knew a wren

who knew Colette. She huddles
on the cobbles — listens to the morse

of the city's skulls, watches bridges
fling their sturdy spans across the Seine

dares to believe these pulsing
stones could be her home.

La Goutte d'Or

was a droplet of exotic clinging to the rim of Paris. Its sound was yellow and praise-like, its smell coriander and bodies. Pâtisseries glowed with sugary saffron, ruby and peridot. I fell in love with the concept of couscous. Pain arabe tasted like unformed memories. From the windows of my corner flat I could *I spy* all day.

I was held across the sea, powerless to return, and when I came again with my dusty cloak and little feet there was no corner. I ask a man and he says *razed, rebuilt.* All the houses sleek and dirty modern;

but my crooked floor
    but my roachy stairs
        but my crumbly walls

La Goutte d'Or is an area in the 18th arrondissement.

Zuihitsu: the year of the thief

You are staying in a hotel near St Placide, looking for work. During the first week your watch, grandmother's cameo ring, St Christopher and some money disappear from your bedside table while you sleep. You tell the manager. He says his hotel is not a brothel, he will have to tell the police about all the men who visit your room if you report the theft. You have no idea what he is talking about. You are from Surrey, still more or less a virgin. The manager has a big tall head like a cartoon baddie. Your room is self-locking. The only way to access it from the outside is with a key.

*

You hook up with a band of outsiders who meet in a café in the suburbs like the one in *Bande à Part*. You have become Godardian with a haircut like Anna Karina. You leave the hotel and sleep on floors, cushions, random beds. You have invented couch surfing.

*

Companion…those you choose to break bread with.

*

Jean-Paul rents a flat with enough room for an extra mattress on the floor. There are planks of wood on trestles for a table; running water. You have no chairs. You have no work. Your money is running out. Opposite is a grocer's. You steal bread. French bread is not easy to steal, particularly baguettes, but the grocer's shop displays large wheels of *pain arabe* on outside displays. Wide and flat as trenchers, they could absorb the juices of all the food you can't cook. You perfect a swift grab, hide, turn and sprint. The grocers are friendly and tolerant although for a long time you believe you have the makings of a master thief.

*

In *Les Misérables,* Jean Valjean is sentenced to five years' imprisonment for stealing a loaf of bread for his dying nephew. Harvest failures. Food shortages. High prices for bread. These were the backdrop to Revolution. Rioters hanged a baker when he had no bread to sell. Now there are strict laws about price and quality.

'Richness and poverty must both disappear from the government of equality. It will no longer make a bread of wheat for the rich and a bread of bran for the poor. All bakers will be held, under the penalty of imprisonment, to make only one type of bread: The Bread of Equality.' (1793 Convention)

*

You have always been a bit in love with Jean Gabin. It was said that all men wanted to be his friends and all women his lovers. You wonder if Depardieu was ever considered the new Gabin... Both Gabin and Depardieu have played Jean Valjean. But Depardieu has renounced his French citizenship (he might be a citizen of Dubai) and praises Putin, whose war against Ukraine, the sixth largest producer of wheat, will send bread prices rocketing.

*

Patrick is bored and you are unemployed. You go to a department store, probably Tati. He nominates you his lookout and steals lots of cheap jewellery that looks as if it would make your skin blacken and itch. You remember he gave you a replacement watch after the St Placide incident. He looks a bit like Jean-Paul Belmondo. You worry what your next lookout role might be.

*

You read that Japanese culinary students have baked loaves of bread, some white, some black (coloured with cocoa powder). The loaves have been cut into 2000 slices and used to make a mosaic of the Mona Lisa.

*

There is no such thing as a free lunch, unless you know Pierre, whose company plies him with luncheon vouchers. You meet once a week. He uses the vouchers to buy two *formules*. You eat brains in grey gravy followed by tarte tatin. Every *formule* comes with a small basket of chewy bread.

14

Sometimes when you exchange *bisous* (two in Paris), his lips stray out of the designated area towards the dry corners of your mouth.

*

You own two pairs of jeans which belonged to your younger brother's best friend. In the flea market you buy a man's checked flannel shirt. You have invented grunge.

*

You are fattening like Hansel on your diet of stolen bread and cheap Monoprix camembert. Zips are your enemy. You see your reflection in the Seine, how the ripples roll. You are witch. You are Gretel.

*

Recette: Pain arabe
Mélangez bien la semoule, la levure et la farine, puis ajoutez l'huile d'olive, le sel et enfin l'eau petit à petit, jusqu'à former une pâte bien épaisse en pétrissant. Si votre pâte colle trop, rajoutez un peu de farine et pétriez.
Formez des petites boules de pâte (si trop grosses, la cuisson risque d'être difficile) et les posez sur une plaque avec du papier sulfurisé. Laissez reposer une heure sur une source tiède recouvert d'un tissu humidifié, ou dans un four légèrement préchauffé à 75°c.
Après le temps de pause, saupoudrez d'un peu de semoule fine et enfournez à 210°c pendant 20 minutes. C'est prêt lorsque le pain sonne creux.

*

You don't like crusty bread. It reminds you of fire, char. You remember the Great Fire of London started in a bakery. You would love the kind of mother who would cut off your crusts, make you thin cucumber sandwiches, who doesn't say how much she wants a daughter with curly hair...

*

The bande à part have regular get-togethers where everyone brings a dish they have made. You take stolen bread.

*

In eighteenth century King's Lynn a 7-year-old boy and his sister were hanged for stealing bread.

*

In Père Lachaise cemetery you meet a couple from Argentina who love Borges. Is this a cliché? *Did you know,* you say, *that after Germany, Chile has the highest consumption of bread per capita worldwide?* They smile and say *si, si.*

*

You have little memory of what you drank in Paris but do remember craving tea. Hot, strong, milky with sugar. This was before the days when you acquired a taste for strong black coffee. You start going to the cafés on the Champs Elysées, particularly the Georges V. You are part feral, anti-establishment, this arrondissement is your enemy. You always order a pot of tea, always sit on the *terrasse*, the most expensive area. You stare at the heavy white china pot. It has an insignia. The teabag is limp with smudgy stale dust, the perfect accompaniment to the 1970s. It arrives on a separate saucer like a VIP. It colours the water light amber. If you add milk, it goes grey. You are the worst kind of watercolourist. You wait until the waiters go inside, stride off without paying. You think all your actions are revolutionary, every thought a happening.

*

You don't yet know you are a writer even though your words pour into diaries and letters. A rolled up piece of white bread can erase pencil marks. French exercise books are squared, not lined. This gives you writer's block. You were always crap at maths.

*

Claude Monet — Still Life with Bottle, Carafe, Bread, and Wine, c. 1862/1863
Light falls on a rumpled linen table-cloth. The walls are whitewashed, a little grubby. On the cloth is a straight-sided carafe of brandy, next to it a bulbous

carafe of water, a bevelled wine-glass, a re-corked bottle of unlabelled red wine, two thirds drunk. The white, uneven-edged plate is next to a sharp knife. On the plate a bright slice of cheese, some crumbs. A baguette lies next to the plate. Cut in half with one half intact, one half part-eaten. On the wall is the bottom edge of what is clearly an impressionist painting.

*

You dream of that painting; of bread and waterlilies.

*

Tati was a famous, and very cheap, department store in Barbès.
Bande à Part (1964) is a film directed by Jean-Luc Godard. It translates as Band of Outsiders.

formule: fixed menu
bisous: kisses

Mon Cher Lucien

She buys a thin, creased postcard in the Llandudno flea market. On the back is a red one-penny stamp from the reign of Edward VII and a block of cramped handwriting in French congratulating *Mon cher Lucien* on his progress in English. *Mon cher Lucien* lives in a street in Paris obscured by a postmark. The writer, whose name is indecipherable, talks of having taken a walk with Miss Burgess. *Almost me,* she thinks as she pays the wide and confiding stallholder. *What's on the back's more important than what's on the front,* he tells her, although she is rather taken with the naïve watercolour depiction of the Serpentine in Hyde Park. *Once,* he continues, leaning forward, *I found a box of postcards at an auction. As I read each one I realised they were all from myself.* She is unsettled by so many coincidences and that night dreams of *Mon cher Lucien.* He is on a bicycle and looks like Henri Serre in *Jules et Jim.* He cycles off before she can tell him about the postcard. The next night she dreams she is standing on the street with the obliterated name. She shouts, *Mon cher Lucien!* and three men turn round. A cloud, black and heavy as an inkblot, darkens the street.

Jules et Jim (1962) is a film directed by François Truffaut.

Marché aux Puces, Porte de Vanves

a set of pocket-sized silver dogs — slits in their backs to hold guests' name cards
a hand-held fire-shield to prevent ruddiness
an ancient fan, silk peeling from its backing like birch bark
a lace baby's bonnet, pristine, threaded with pink silk ribbon
an eighteenth-century breast pump, crystal
a tiny purse, heavy metallic thread, to hold a coin for a tram & a pot of rouge
a scrap of wallpaper, faded cerise
a bag of orphaned buttons
a studio photograph of a fin-de-siècle beauty: impossible waist, kissable shoulders
I look into her eyes and know she has survived the oldest story in the world

The Paris Project — Cento I

He sees the quartier caught unawares —
moonlight on the roofs of the tall house,
two lovers standing by the glow
of the chestnut seller's brazier.
Fingers stained darker than his hair,
they danced some more…reminded
each other of things they had seen and felt
the night before.
His hair was cropped army short.
The cinema was a dungeon —
it was a Kieślowski movie.
All of the sadness of the city came suddenly —
the marble-topped tables, the smell of early morning.

*The Paris Project — an undertaking to read as many books about Paris or with Paris in the title as I could in one year in order to produce a series of Centos. Cento I consists of word clusters from Geoff Dyer's **Paris Trance**, Graham Robb's **Parisians** and Ernest Hemingway's **A Moveable Feast**.*

Où est le Métro s'il-vous-plait?

She wants to write a *poème de métro*, like the OuLiPo:
- between stops think of your lines
- only write when the train is stationary
- if the train stops between stations decide on your strategy
- sometimes certain letters are banned — eg. *write an ode without using O* —

but

      on the elevated sections she forgets to focus
distracted by winter sunlight on Haussmann stone
people doing ordinary things behind grimy windows,
      even boiling pasta seems exotic in Paris
      a knob of butter, a grate of hard cheese et voilà!
There's the Eiffel Tower revealing different sections as the train chunters by —
      an industrial striptease.

The Métro is a melting pot, a shoulder-rubbing nearness.
She sniffs her sleeve — a faint trace of last night's omelette.
As the carriage warms she detects couscous, spices, hunger…
      She maps above-ground in her head *now we are under the Seine — in Seine!*

The next day, there's a strike, the Métro is closed.
She is mesmerised by the art nouveau curves of the entrance at Abbesses,
beautiful as a brooch.
A carrier bag drifts along the pavement, a curious shade of blue.
      Hello blue, she thinks, remembers the hyacinth walls of another life
      as if paint could make things right
      banish the blue-bound threat of bible
      blue, blue, her favourite colour inside and out.
      Once she loved the idea of a boy in perfect powder-blue velvet —
      a pocket brother — well-behaved.
      She wears a lapis lazuli ring so shiny she wants to smell it,
      smell it like the little bluebells streaked with white
      struggling between gravestones

she remembers a sad blue balloon
sagging in a wilt of stretchmarks &
common blues fluttering from clifftops
like confetti in reverse.
Once there was the exact blue of a beaded necklace
& how it broke, filled her breasts with ice.

She opens her eyes. The Métro is still a conundrum *'1 in 4 trains running'*
the best it can do.

A sparrow tilts his head, pecks at a fleck of brioche.

Darkness falls, a slow blindfolding.

Tomorrow, she thinks, *tomorrow.* She will follow all the rules. In addition, she
will not use the letters

m e t r o

The OuLiPo (Ouvroir de Littérature Potentielle — workshop for potential literature) were a loose group of writers and mathematicians, founded by Raymond Queneau and François Le Lionnais in 1960 and included Georges Perec and Italo Calvino. They enjoyed using constrained writing techniques and the poème de métro is one such constraint.

Paris is a blonde

and I am stalking her
                              I shake my umbrella
and yesterday's rain clings to its folds

                 today she traces the phantom river from the 13ème
rainbowed with tannery trash   tapestry dye

she boards a train at the Gare de Vincennes
                         alights at La Tour du Philosophe
she thinks   therefore I am

Paris is a blonde   a lèche-vitrine de l'inconscient
                         at Café Riche she orders un café allongé
we no longer have a reflection

there is the coincidence of the abattoirs de Vaugirard
                         waters running red as the Bièvre

it's *pile ou face* and I go left and she goes right
                         but I am still behind her

night is a monster nocturne sauvage
            what are the aesthetics of this wasteland? I ask
je suis un collage, she shrugs
            oh meet me tomorrow at the Château Tremblant
for what I love most is the instability of your raincoat

*Inspired by a line from the song "Ça c'est Paris" written by Lucien Boyer and Jacques Charles
and sung by Mistinguett; also inspired by Sophie Calle's artwork, particularly "Suite
Venitienne". The places cited in the poem no longer exist.*

I find a photo of my imaginary parents in the Paris flea-market

Her hair is in victory rolls; he has a soldier's haircut and eyes full of unliberated stories. What price a family photograph? The stallholder won't negotiate, even when I explain who they are, and that, yes, I know the dates don't tally, but I'm prepared to be much older. It's worth it to be French.

Did you know they only stopped serving alcohol to the under-14s in French school canteens in 1956? And that's why I'm a connoisseur of all things Beaujolais. In a shoebox somewhere there's a photo of me with black school stockings and black-stained lips.

Then I see a photo of my imaginary cousin. She was there, with her Bardot hair, when my voice sprang from the bear-trap of adolescence, pinning men to the sweating walls of Paris jazz-clubs with its honey-pot vowels. We would jive until sunrise in mini-dresses of orange and navy blue crimplene with giant white buttons and oh, the glorious intimacy of our bones...

Discovering Calentica (1986)

I'm an Assistante at Collège Les Mousseaux in Villepinte. *That's where that teacher was raped,* says my friend's abusive boyfriend but I can tell by his little eyes that he lies. The kids lock me in cupboards, push me down stairs. One stabs the head-teacher. There are sirens.

One evening the boys circle me on mopeds as I stroll to the RER. The streets empty. There is a blink of tumbleweed in the distance. My thumbs are alert on my hips, touching the folds of make-believe holsters, sharp keys threaded through trigger-happy fingers. The mopeds break formation with a reluctant whine.

After school I go to Nicole's tiny flat to teach English to her sons. We met queueing for free ballet tickets. Nicolas is three. He parrots me in perfect English. Michel looks like Joe 90. Pascal is a prankster. Patrice gives me his homework to do. Jean-Paul blushes every time he says *Suzanne.* I am beguiled by these boys; they are like a manual — *Five Stepping Stones to Positive Manhood.*

Nicole is fierce, with an intriguing accent. *Pied noir.* She regales her husband with the exotica of my vegan diet. He watches soaps and smokes.

French markets are full of purple peppers shiny as amethysts; bitter ivory-leaved endives; frilly lettuces bigger than dinner-plates. But on menus there's barely a légume to crunch on.

In the benign matriarchy of her tiny kitchen, Nicole cooks me sweet couscous with almonds and dates. Or calentica — street-food in the banlieue. Chick pea flour, olive oil, water, harissa, cumin — beaten and baked. Nicole speaks faster than she beats, zigzagging questions across the kitchen, *Il est beau, ton Jules?*

One night we have free tickets for the Moulin Rouge. I squirm as the topless dancers jiggle on stage — it's like watching a sex scene with my mum.

I still make calentica. As I whisk, I imagine Nicole reigning over a kitchen full of steam and clapping grandsons.

RER: regional railway
pied noir: French people who lived in Algeria during colonial rule and returned to France after Algeria was declared independent
Il est beau, ton Jules?: is your boyfriend good-looking?

Paris is a Palimpsest

she thinks, reading today's menu, chalked over the ghost of last week's *formule*
posters on lampposts flake like wallpaper, reveal a slither of Jane Avril's scissoring legs;
can she peel her skin back to the days when she was understudying her future self?
here's the épicerie opposite her old flat, a slippage of cantilevered vegetables,
pears smeared with choosy fingerprints;
the blue 4CV with a dent the size of a knee, the wing mirror where she used to check her face;
the past is like the scurry of a mouse in a still room, she thinks, *a reminder you live with the uninvited;*
sandalled feet, running backwards;
soupe du jour, s'il vous plait

Cinematic

"Cinema is the most beautiful fraud in the world." Jean-Luc Godard

I am wearing moodiness and a trench coat;
the canal is experimenting with greys —

its rain-rippled water, a reel of slatey silk,
makes a shifting mosaic of my face.

I drink coffee that tastes like punishment,
learn these apartments were once cowsheds.

Swans are gathering by the ancient edges
of Île St Louis, the tips of their feathers

the dirty yellow of ageing limestone;
the river is the colour of falling leaves.

There are too many mirrors in bars, my tongue
is coated with vin chaud and everywhere there's

another one of me. The Tunnel des Tuileries
is a cacophony of street art. I want to stay

in this darkling place, tag my name,
reluctant Persephone, stubborn Eurydice.

At Deyrolle, a butterfly's vivid indigo grace
disintegrates behind glass, my fingers brush

a lioness's whiskers and I have fallen in love again
with Sacré Coeur, gleaming like salt in moonlight.

Deyrolle is a famous taxidermist showroom on the Left Bank, which featured in Woody Allen's film "Midnight in Paris".

Mapping It

After the second power-cut between *Bréguet Sabin* and *Charonne* the women open their handbags and begin to make an underground palace. One discovers she has bought fifteen postcards of the same painting. Another says she understands finally that her lover will always be a photograph torn in half. A man opens his wallet, unfolds a picture of Juliette Greco and spittles it to the dark window.

They eat chewing gum, nicotine patches and indigestion pills. They use the scratch of the double seats against the itch of fleabites. When the train finally moves again it's a Tuesday and they get as far as *Abbesses* where the lips of martyrs whisper miracles like gossip.

Hunger is the gap between the train and the platform edge. A pale woman with Brigitte Bardot hair spins stories as they pass through *Sully Morland*. Tales of blind silkworms and their kingdom. She asks, *Am I the only one who thinks they are the only one screaming?*

Reincarnation as the Eiffel Tower

I was made
on the eighth day
out of the rib of revolution
where scar tissue aches
when I sway

I bedazzle the night with my swathes
of bling, reflected in the convex shine
of a thousand tourists' eyes

I swear I'm bending closer to the Seine
seeking my dandy reflection
as the sun's alchemy transforms dull waters
to a horizontal Hall of Mirrors

I have renounced my skin for gleam
my wrought joints swell and sweat
in August's heat
and I long
for snow and monochrome.

On sunny days the Eiffel Tower bends up to 18cm away from the sun.

A Thanksgiving Dinner as described in *The Alice B Toklas Cookbook*

Let me come to your laden table, bearing the gift of my orphaned life for you to host in your *salon des refusés*. Introduce me to your servants, who are all called Jeanne, who are all related, who cannot cook.

Let me peer under this tablecloth for I fear I have brought my skeletons with me. Oh Miss Getrude Stein, let me speak to you about this chair:

This chair does not connect mustard and is a change with nickel and probably cushion azure so blind and not a furniture, yes let's.

The turkey is legless — Jeanne has served herself first in her sacrilegious kitchen. Oh Alice, these creamed potatoes are sublime and cornbread stuffing dances from your little hands. Let me stay under your table with its altar-cloth of fringed oxblood. I will lick your toes and eat your crumbs and identify great painters by the state of their shoes.

Excavation

hidden rivers   invisible as bone marrow   flow like the Bièvre /   your blood
remembers /   a soldier   unhinged eyes   live grenade over his bed   in
breath   out breath   roof becomes sky /   what does blackness smell like
dark vinegary taste of absence /   Neuchâtel   a waiter gives you free wine
a kiss like a Hollywood cliché   your train pulls out /   other skies emptying
before your wavering gaze /   ashy ghosts fleeing   on screen   off screen
on a loop /   Clapham Junction   a busker   cool hat   battered guitar   his
bedsit   coins buried in overflowing ashtrays /   bridges burnt   you learn
to walk on water /   Rome   a guileless American   sandals sliding in imperial
dust /   Paris   a gap where you used to live   the city disembowelling its
memories of you /   a beautiful boy on the Métro   adored for two stops
gone like a crop-haired Eurydice [...]

The Bièvre is one of Paris's hidden, paved over rivers, like the Fleet in London.

The Artificial Parisienne

envie the Parisienne inside me bloomed the day I realised de visiter Paris
ses sites I didn't live in Mill Street's suburbia but on the rue du Moulin historiques
mais également and my name was Suzanne des lieux plus confidentiels?
je suis votre guide my paper dolls spent their flimsy lives je vous accompagne dans
votre découverte de Paris dressed as stereotypes Que suis-je?
Parisienne et guide I thought streetwalker chic was de rigueur je vous emmène

the sky in Paris is different
tattooed with Eiffel Tower
domes spires
defiance of Montparnasse
odd low glimpse of gold

à la découverte the Parisienne inside me is shrug and pout des quartiers emblématiques
et des lieux qui font she gets all the jokes in *Un gars, une fille* charme magique
la capitale before the subtitles des rues pittoresques
des quartiers she is a black and white gitane contrail femme fatale à l'esprit de village
des parcs to a Bechet soundtrack et des jardins
she has three berets from Pigalle on three hooks
red white blue

the moon in Paris is different
its raison d'être to crown the dome of Sacré Coeur
one night I dream I climb the scaly tiles
plunge my arms deep into brightness

des passages niches the Parisienne inside me is au coeur de la ville
je vous fais partager too many little black dresses mes connnaissances
mais aussi a surfeit of Colette mes bonnes adresses
coups de coeur the hiss and pull of accordion un voyage gastronomique
et culturel to Belleville chansons des lieux méconnus
la tristesse

the trees in Paris are different
their heartwood bears the scream of revolution
the thud of Occupation
leaf-dust scatters
inhabits my lungs like remembrance

conseillé même aux âmes the Parisienne inside me les plus fragiles
cette visite is high-voiced mime-hands peut se faire en toutes
saisons   pénétrez vowel sounds requiring dans des profondeurs
vous passerez devant expensive red lipstick les puits des carriers

the stones in Paris are different
the city has disembowelled itself
to create a maze of dreams and light

vous entrez the Parisienne inside me is leather-jacketed dans la nécropole
pixie-cut anarchist graffiti artist
un ossuaire of the underground qui contient
les restes de and like the ancient Kings of France 6 millions de parisiens
who distributed their remains
la danse macabre between three churches la marche funèbre
cette visite I will spray-paint a tower for my febrile heart at Barbès vous permettra
d'observer avec by the clatter of métro and market quel soin
quasi artistique chalk my entrails on the quais les os
ont été rangés of Canal St Martin une pensée particulière
sera adressée jettison my knotted bones at the bend in the Seine devant le sarcophage
du poète where Notre Dame spews her buttresses like fountains of stone inconnu

This poem is embedded in found texts from the internet aimed at tourists wishing to visit Paris.

She is the woman I should have been
for Jean Hall (née Pestell)

The hour I am born, mewling, into the wrong life,
she's eavesdropping on Sartre and de Beauvoir
in the days when the streets of Paris
are a showcase and women match
their dogs to their furs.

This woman I should have been
is petite, sophisticated —
her dark delinquent fall of hair
reminds men of that actress
who's always on the tip of their tongue;
her lips taste of Nuits St Georges
drunk straight from the bottle.

The day they transport Jean Moulin
to the Panthéon, she's in the crowd
as it susurrates down the boulevard
leaning into the wind to catch
Malraux' homage… *résistons résistons…*

This woman I should have been
samples all 127 available cheeses,
drinks Marie Brizard, holds her nose
at the odour colouring the air
over the pavement pissoirs.

Her flatmates fight over a handsome
clichéd man who takes her
to Olympia, kisses her too hard
too long to a Charles Aznavour chanson.

This woman I should have been
leaves Paris for Spain to whisper
in Hemingway's ear while I start school
and begin to learn French
as if I know who I am.

Le Petit Prince

I buy *Le Petit Prince* from a grumpy bouquiniste with intellectual hair and eyes the colour of the Seine on cloudless days. *It's one of the ten most popular books in the world,* he says, as if I have hesitated. Sometimes I hear the words *dessine-moi un mouton* in my dreams, wonder if I've counted badly drawn sheep to fall asleep. Today the Seine is a sleepy ribbon glinting in unexpected sunshine. I take *Le Petit Prince* to the cinema, the one with the cobbled courtyard and Wallace fountain. I can hear his endless questions rustling the pages as I try to concentrate on a labyrinthine film noir. He is the child I still am, so thirsty for life that I'm living two; never able to swim off the urban grit that silts the core of me in my little village by the sea.

The bouquinistes have plied their trade of second-hand and antiquarian books from booths along the Seine for centuries.

This is where

Two streets away lives the me I left behind in 1979, tongue full of slang, heart full of salt. I could have been the woman who grabbed my arm for balance in the métro yesterday, stringy with nerves and apology.

I tune into the lilt of the streets of Barbès. If I lean at a 77° angle from my window I can see Sacré Coeur across the roof-scape, lit by a parenthetical moon. This is where Duchess purred her way into the soul of Thomas O'Malley in *The Aristocats* via Eva Gabor's silky ventriloquism. Listen, and you might hear Scat Cat and his matted, furball-chomping crew jazz up the skyline on this cool January night.

In the distance Hemingway roars, *Paris belongs to me and I belong to this notebook and this pencil!*

I close the shutters, feel cold pen strokes on my skin, somewhere someone is writing my other story.

Barbès Rochechouart is a lively area in the 18th arrondissement.

I am building Paris in my bedroom

First, I cut a string of paper dolls from a back-copy of *Le Monde* — such a city needs a population of a certain kind of girl. Here's one who arrived in Paris for the first time, shiny, innocent, and left with *je ne sais quoi* and a fringe like Juliette Greco.

I am building Paris in my bedroom. From leftover Lego I snap Notre Dame into higgledy shape, balance a flimsy girl on the Quai aux Fleurs. She easily answers the question *Where were you when...?* for she is always in Paris when someone famous dies. She will speak of the friend who died with unwritten dances still inside, how she sat in shock in her Bastille flat, brimming with unwept tears.

In my dreams I'm lost in Montreuil's labyrinthine *murs de pêche*, hands a mess of clawed juice, crushed kernel; or I'm deep in the catacombs — conducting a pyramid of skulls grinning dusty harmonies to regretful songs.

I am building Paris in my bedroom. See, here's the Eiffel Tower fashioned from a cat's cradle lifted from my lover's fingers in 1981. Today I plan to craft the silhouette of Sacré Coeur, tear off a wavering girl to place on the steps. She's a girl who had a doll's house but no idea of home; a girl who thinks she sees angels, bought a penny string of beads and named them rosary. A girl who looked for love in a scavenged prayer-book.

I am building Paris in my bedroom. Look, I'll put a girl here on Pont St Michel cupping the silk of the Seine like a sacrament to fill her home with light, Gallic shrugs, the joyful lather of French soap, unexpected brioche crumbs between the sofa cushions. This girl knows she's a cliché in her belted mac, angled beret, quick slick of *Rouge Allure*; some days she is noir to her soul — *résistez, résistez!* A girl can be too cool you know, instead of strutting the streets as if she belongs she should kiss the platform of the Gare du Nord, ecstatic, papal.

I am building Paris in my bedroom. Here are the chaotic market stalls of Barbès clustered under my bed. I fashion them the old way with matchsticks and twine, colour in polystyrene food with felt-tip pens. The trick is to not want to be somewhere else, not to crave the cracked skin of a perfect baguette. This girl, this girl, when she tries to speak her mouth is dry with the rust of unsaid vowels.

Bagatelle

O I'm right behind you Mr Beau de l'Air
with your bag full of chalk and cheese
yes I'm right behind you like a child
Qu'elle heure est-il M. Le Loup?
with my pigeon steps   my fairy steps   my tippy toes
giant steps hors de question
with all this flin flan flânerie
O botanist of the sidewalk
what's so interesting about dust and shit
all I want is my morning baguette
plucked warm from the rack
sweating a little in its paper wrap
O folie de baguette   sometimes I think I've made you up
with your pickable crust   craquelure for my tartine lust
I want you soft white belly up slathered in pêche

O I'm still behind you Mr Beau de l'Air
with your sac plein de craie et fromage.
Is that a turtle you're leading along the trottoir?
Do I note a swagger   albeit slow
a little whoosh from side to side?
Well there's been window-shopping at the quincaillerie
a bit of dribbling outside the confiserie
some finger and thumb work at the fruiterie
but all I want is my warm baguette
leavened from poverty   proved in Terror
shouting *egalité!* from the top of the streets
stackable as firewood   former splendour
shrunk to less than the length of my arm
O tearable tempter   sauce sopper
upside down for the Executioner
inspirer of etiquette & layers of lore
flour salt yeast   your weight dictated
you double in size to fill my mouth

O Monsieur Beau de l'Air   yes I'm still here
in the shadow of your cloak
while you saunter sunny side up
with your panier full of lime and stink
I suspect you're a bit of a badaud under that hat
already drunk on street-life at 8am
O flin flan flânerie you're my subject now
I'm overtaking you   inviting you   disrupting your gaze
now it's click clack paddywack to the boulangerie
yes once I get my hands on that thick baguette
it's breakfast with Beau de l'Air   ready or not

In Which A Middle-Aged Woman in Primark Jeans Denies Her Invisibility

to be read in a breathless rush

Can that be me, mon dieu, c'est pas vrai, in the LBD (c'est le dernier cri) that I've always craved, grazing slim knees and oh! slim legs, oh yes this vitrine is loving me — is that a fascinator I spy, rakish angle, speckled veil trailing over one eye? Now over the road in confident strides in my little black traffic-stopper my well-judged heels *yeah right, connasse to you too mate!* Tu vois how my middle fingernail is a perfect coral blush and Louboutin's window, well, c'est très utile to paint a pout in *Rouge Interdit* and oh! par hasard here's my charming friend tout à Givenchy *mwah mwah, oui, oui, à bientôt chérie.*

Now my rump is pumped so I try a little BCBG sashay down the rue St Honoré where a cool lycéenne with a cool teenage stare bursts my rêverie with one slow blink of her Rimmeled eyes, one long swish of her nouvelle-vague hair, one nonchalantly implied *dégage* and   I'm simply not there.

BCBG is French slang for bon chic, bon genre (good style, good attitude) to describe a bourgeois lifestyle. This was quickly corrupted into beau cul, belle gueule (nice ass, pretty face).

An LBD is a Little Black Dress.

The Paris Project — Cento II

Feet in both worlds, I'm a conduit
hands on my belly, howling like a dog.
We lived in silk kimonos
steps raising a fine dust,
I sought to be nothing for everyone
long shadows across the courtyard of Hotel Sully
powdery plaster spitting from the stone arch —
I cannot remember the name of the street
little round tables dot the semicircle of cobbled stones
hazy globes of light
the hoarse notes of her song.
Sirens wail in the distance
I watch them march and stand
light candles, look bewildered —
a circle both can and can't be closed

Word clusters from Cara Black's crime series **Murder in the Marais, Murder in Belleville, Murder in the Latin Quarter, Murder in the Sentier,** *George Orwell's* **Down and Out in London and Paris** *and Andrew Gallix's anthology* **We'll Never Have Paris.**

Apprenticeship

a hot shed in the Negev
      bunching gypsophila stems
      one two three   tie
      throbbing lament of Arabic pop
      hotskinned tomatoes
      bursting in my city mouth

 and Paris where I teach
      a man with no voice-box
      to speak English
      in syllables like centimes
      bouncing on the zinc counter
      of *Le Bistrot du Coin*

an old people's home near Afullah
      glimpses of camp tattoos
      Hillel smears his beautiful shit
      on the wall   on himself
      Rahel cries her weight in tears
      I empty yeasty yellow-full catheters
      master the art of bedpan

and Paris   manual typewriter
      Amnesty International intern
      the clunk of ink-clogged keys
      I conjure words without looking
        e l e c t r o d e
      long reports on abuse   torture
      I'm too naïve for this
      my hands smell metallic

      like the thick twisted chains
      we gripped to loop the loop
      swinging so high the roofs of old town
      become ground
      back when I was six   an improbable girl
      and work was what my father did
      his saw piling rills of dust at my feet.

In Printemps Department Store

A sleety April shower drives me in,
past the soldiers on the wet street,
the bag-searchers at the doors.
I escalate up six floors of opulence,
order a jug of *chocolat onctueux*
under a stained glass dome
higher than I can tilt my head.

It reminds me of Kirsten Dunst
in *Marie Antoinette* — surrounded
by pyramids of shoes like sugared almonds,
halls of mirrors reflecting an infinite catwalk,
cascades of champagne, and cake,
layered and extravagant as wigs.

This is how it begins, confides Marie as I take another sip,
shopping lists growing longer, longer
than the sum of my days…
The solace of silk and velvet, the heart-flutter
of new shoes, the best pastries rotting
my weak-willed teeth, my play kingdom
spreading like mould at the end of Louis' careful gardens,
unfinished, a whole age lost under a falling blade.

And perhaps this is how it will end for me,
a sudden shattering,
high heels whirling past like multi-coloured spines,
silk tearing and fluttering in a rainbow of rags;
glass — royal blue, gold, terracotta, peacock,
raining down on my pretty neck.

Marie Antoinette (2006) is a film directed by Sofia Coppola.

The Distant Place

I am travelling between antonyms
my absence a chalk outline
an unpaid coffee   a mis-pronounced vowel

I carry the distant place
when I'm in the near place
light-weight freight discreet tattoo

my skin tastes of the distant place
my tongue always on the brink
                              of naming

La Charlotte de l' Île

Imagine the most perfect chocolate shop, like a glowing page in a child's favourite pop-up book; florentines, madeleines, bonbons, tartes, anthropomorphic teapots, china cows and startled owls; chocolate pulled like taffy into shining fairy tales. A little black book, word-of-mouth, secretive shop run by other-worldly women. Bohemian. Lots of purple. A shop that smells of wishes and heartsease. And if you could place this chocolaterie anywhere in the world, it would be Paris. And if you could place it anywhere in Paris, it would be on Île St Louis. Et voilà, here it is, exactly as you imagined it, at 24, rue St Louis en l'Île.

You go there three times a week for three seasons, sip mint tea, Arabic coffee and chocolat à l'ancienne from fragile handle-less cups in the tiny back room. There are chandeliers and a ringing dinging baroque till. The women sing pastries to life and dream up new shows for the wide-eyed marionettes strung from the beams with the drying herbs. You write letters and read letters and weep. You are poor with tiny writing, limited paper, a careful pile of francs. One day you open a letter and a wish is granted, pouf! just like that you are magicked away to a different life where you undergo a strange long ritual of forgetting.

When you reappear, with crisp euros and good shoes, you experience the worst kind of magic trick — a silk scarf has been laid over your most precious memory and *abracadabra* here's a grubby, amazed pigeon with palsied feet. Someone has scooped out all the spells, apothecary jars, filigree chocolate, and deposited plastic chairs and cheap veneer where once was battered patina.

You become a hopeless humble pilgrim, catching at the fragments of long-torn letters:
dearest   darling   miss you   I am so cold   the coffee here is strong and stops me dreaming   sometimes I tell the marionettes my secrets   there are splinters

Flâneuse

It's 1:15 in Le Polidor and there's a man as drunk
as a Hemingway quote, a woman layering on
the reddest lipstick, *on ne sait jamais...*
I pay and stroll to St Sulpice where the faithful tourists
gaze up, seeking light, cracking the da Vinci code.

In the Jardins de Luxembourg there's a fleet of ducklings
on the pond and boats racing with faded sails in Seurat colours.
I watch *Le Vieux Château* at the Théâtre des Marionettes
on a hard slatted bench and the kids' faces haven't changed
in sixty years since Antoine and René skipped school in *Les 400 Coups*.
Guignol still has shiny black hair, apple cheeks, swivelly eyes,
he's still terrified of everything: *Behind you! Bats! Spiders!
Robbers! On your HEAD!*

Back in the sunlight there are elegant women on metal chairs
reading Proust, Henry James, Malraux; there are no dogs.
I head for the Seine, walk along the quais to the Pont des Invalides
past soggy pizza picnics, one-tune buskers strumming Bob Dylan,
women with mouths that can only be French.
Here's extravagant curlicued Pont Alexandre III, the Eiffel Tower
stabbing the sky.

Up Rue François 1er to the Champs Elysées,
a half-circle round the Arc de Triomphe to Cinéma Mac-Mahon
to watch *How Green Was My Valley* and I cry
whenever hardship comes or a miner dies,
go to the loo where Jean Seberg climbed through the window
in *Breathless* to escape the cops in their too-small hats,
their too-dark glasses.

When I come out it's still light, every corner smells of lily-of-the-valley,
it's the first of May and all the cars of Paris are blowing their horns
in an offbeat city symphony.

The Cemeteries of Paris

Le Cimetière du Père Lachaise
She's not surprised to find Kurt Cobain by Jim Morrison's grave, or as close as she can get to the love-locked loved-up barriers hung with signs instructing BREAK ON THROUGH TO THE OTHER SIDE! No, not surprised, even though he's been dead for over 25 years. They're both in the *27 Club* after all. She's 62 and confident she's not cursed. He's a pale cliché of himself, unplugged. *I cried when you died, oh beautiful boy.*
After she's visited her regulars — a madeleine for Proust, pink roses for Piaf, a quick obeisance at Chopin's heartless monument, *Rouge Coco* kisses for Oscar — she sees Kurt again, pretending he has a game-plan, exploring the bullet holes on Le Mur des Fédérés. She takes his hands. Reads her past in his smooth palms.

Offerings
métro tickets to pay the ferryman
potatoes and pumpkins for hungry ghosts
pencils, sharpened for all the things you forgot to mention
stones balanced on grave-rims
hey you, just passing   again
lipstick kisses, slick over marble, like tiny flames
finger-marks on the grilles of portals   *push me pull you*

Le Cimetière Russe de Ste-Geneviève-des-Bois

Once upon a time there was a graveyard where exiles and emigrés gathered, their diamonds all unsewn, to gossip beneath soil coiled with birch roots.

Open the icon window in the headstone — light a candle for Ivan Mozzhukhin. See how bluebirds pattern the air for Olga Preobrajhenskaya. Watch Andrei Tarkovsky direct his final masterpiece — polished granite, falling maple leaves. Lay your head on the kaleidoscope shimmer covering Nureyev. Hum him into deeper sleep, long bones cool and calm as folded wings.

Once upon a time there was a graveyard glowing like an amber room in a slumbering Winter Palace.

Le Cimetière Monmartre

cats shapeshift between graves   one is afraid of umbrellas
rooks stage shadow theatre with their wings
        perch like dark angels   drink from urns
a small grey van declares
        en-sa-memoire.fr
        votre tombe familiale entretenue et fleurie
        partout en France
will they put fresh coins on your eyes   primp your already gorgeous bones
        will they know how you loved to dance?

between Cimetière Monmartre and Cimetière St Vincent
        she eats a choux à la crème de matcha
                an affirmation of life in two feral bites —

she drinks absinthe for remembrance
        it looks like liquid peridot, tastes like childhood...

Headstones

i. *Napoleon's Balloonist*

she is bright sun and wolf moon
      dizzy with hydrogen
hair a crackling halo
      white empire-line dress   ostrich plumes
she perches in her basket   swaying rooftop cradle
      peels the glow from an orange
watches dusk bleed light from the narrow streets
      she has launched fireworks from her fingertips
Bengal fire for Emperors and Kings
      Then I flew over the Alps, my skin sharp with icicle
she tells the cooling tiles
      she does not know how close she is to death
      how she will fall from her blazing balloon
      a skirted Icarus.

Sophie Blanchard (1778–1819) was the first woman to work as a professional balloonist, at first with her husband and then solo after his death. She plunged to her death when her aerial firework display set her balloon on fire. She is buried in Père Lachaise.

ii. *Gertrude,*

Alice still has your back   sees the wives of geniuses coming
through the gates   reminds you of their names   so when they lay their
stones and flowers and sharpened pencils   you can confound them with
your wit
      Stones on edge of and kettles and pans balancing on the boils
      of many waters   thank you Mrs Wife of Genius

Gertrude Stein (1874–1946), novelist, poet and patron, and Alice B Toklas (1877–1967) were lifelong companions and are buried together in Père Lachaise. Their names are carved on either side of their headstone.

iii. Renée Vivien composes a ghazal for Violet Shillito

I knew at first sight you were the colour of all my heartbeats, Violet,
I wept in woodlands as thoughtless heels crushed modest violets.

When I think of you, Sappho's words fly from my pen like thousands
of urgent migrating birds, for you were my delicious air, Violet.

I didn't realise dying was an art until I tried and failed, needed years
of practice to find your darling, dead, delirious face, ma Violette.

How can I write poems without mentioning these humble flowers,
regal robes, fresh bruises, or the colour of dawn, which is, of course, violet.

When I finally master the trickiest of arts, I am ready with my dying wish,
so here lies *Renée Vivien*, heart stilled at last under a posy of violets.

Renée Vivien (1877–1909) was a British poet who wrote in French. She was in love with her childhood friend, Violet Shillito, who died of tuberculosis in 1901. Vivien is buried in Le Cimetière de Passy.

iv. Agnès Varda

Agnès in your coat of soil
rosy-cheeked matryoshka
widow's grief
held hard & deep
in the smallest doll;
we miss your square hair —
visit you in black & white
& colour;
can you see our
to-ing & fro-ing
in the endless reel
of your afterlife?

Agnès Varda (1928–2019) was a film director, screenwriter, photographer and artist, an important influence on the French New Wave. She was married to fellow director Jacques Demy, who died in 1990. They are buried in the same grave in Le Cimetière du Montparnasse.

v.

a magpie visits
Pearl White in her tomb
of plain black polished granite

(a twisted haiku in 5–5–7)

Pearl White (1889–1938) was a stage and screen actress from the age of six. She was famous for doing her own stunts, particularly in the popular series "The Perils of Pauline". She worked for Pathé, lived in Montparnasse and is buried in Le Cimetière de Passy.

The Animal Cemetery Calls Her Name
(Le Cimetière des chiens, Asnières)

double gates   over-wrought   the bite of lichen on stone
& already I want to cry over these bony little lives

Kiki   Plume   Fétiche   Pignou   Youpi

I envy them tucked tight in their des res
on the wrong side of the Seine
snug in chestnut and pine beds
Hervé's grave holds a bowl of tennis balls
gnawed and licked to baldness
here's *Moustache* who fought by Napoleon
Drapeau who served in the Great War
a line of police dogs obey their final command
near *Rin Tin Tin* — star of the silver screen

Madame Dubois sweeps the gravel
bordering three black marble hearts
one for *Missy* one for *Elvis* one for luck
a tiny headstone declares   *deçue par les humains
jamais par mon chien**

a host of cremated cats nestle
in the columbarium like ashy pigeons

and here's *Barry* the St Bernard who saved forty lives
shot by soldiers who thought him a wolf
his big heart sighing out in the snow
Diesel who died in a terrorist attack
Faust the sheep and *Ezequielle* the tortoise
& rabbits to make the dogs twitch in their sleep

Tipsy   Pluche   Toby   Bobette   Pompon   Troye

I remember the scraggy poodle
my aunt named after me when I was motherless
Suzette
& how perhaps she comforted me
despite the smelliness of her lamby coat
the look of despair in her speechless eyes

*Trans: *disappointed by humans, by my dog — never*

This Place

She watches *Chacun Cherche Son Chat,* set in the Bastille streets of the 90s where she lived in the 80s. When did that place become this place? As Chloe and Djamel search the streaky streets and jagged rooftops for a lost cat, black, with a grey patch, she touches fingertips with an earlier self. *Gris-gris! Gris-gris!* they shout into the thin air between the squeeze-stile alleyways.

Let's play a game, she says, stepping back further — the cat unfound, the cries unheard.

Under her old window (*still there, still square*) on Rue de Lappe she places the not-that-close-by market so she can smell the bruise of orange skin and the rub of mint all day. She moves the chocolatier from Île-St-Louis to the corner opposite, where the bakery was. And why shouldn't she jump cut the dusty obsolescence of never-knew-the-name-of-anyway streets for the sake of a stand-your-spoon-up-in-it hot chocolate? Now she's reburying Piaf, Chabrol, Wilde and Chopin. *We're going to have so much to talk about,* she tells them as they shift their bones and moan under the uneven cobbles near *Le Balajo* and its seedy Monday tea-dances.

Balade of the Fallen

The streets are noir as a Michelle Morgan film
        the plaques of Paris whisper their stories, old and new
                Ne les oublions jamais
how trains became prisons
        the velodrome a holding pen
a rock club a tomb
        the Seine a morgue
how schools forgot the thirteen ways to keep children safe
        how the wall of names shouts its pain
there's a bright new grave in Père Lachaise
        forgotten bullet holes in Rue de Rivoli

A prophetic man under Pont Neuf holds forth to his own echo —
        when she opens her mouth to answer, it is full of plosives.

'Balade' is French for walk/stroll but also sounds very much like 'Ballad'. My soundtrack when writing this was Charlie Haden's 'Ballad of the Fallen', which inspired the title.

Barbès Rochechouart

In the time it takes you to forget and remember
the keys, go up to the flat, return,
your car has become a street stall;
unrolled rugs sold quick-fire on the bonnet,
the brief lean of a prostitute against the door.

The Métro thunders overhead
but I'm trapped inside this quatre-chevaux
like a snail-trailed Dali mannequin.

I hate driving in Paris:
that time the wheel came off
and the axle grooved
a tarmac trench towards the Seine.
The national parking technique
a bumper car parody.

You're back, but now the car won't start,
ten colourful curses later we sit in a couscousserie.
You order a Royale and I remember that speech
in *Pulp Fiction* about Paris,
Big Macs and the metric system.

You tell me that the bridge with all the padlocks
is so heavy with love it's sinking
and buy me a green North African macaroon
although you know I prefer the red ones.

We walk neon-drowned streets,
stop for a kir, find the car's still there.
You pick your teeth in the wing mirror
and I find a centime —
a tiny copper moon in the wet gutter.

Pulp Fiction (1994) is a film directed by Quentin Tarantino.

The Paris Project — Cento III

The sun set orange over the evening city,
he called out of the blue
began to talk about Paris over dinner —
the language was a version of French
the story wasn't a story.
I heard my voice carrying over the crooked rooftops —
a block away a food market was set up
old men in lace caps were selling caftans.
I thought I might be in love with our waiter
we switched our order from coffee to a bottle of red wine
it was near closing time.
We had our own rituals —
he wore his voluminous cape everywhere
told his men to be subversive —
the arrests included married butchers
it was the worst of times.
I thought I was at the top of the Eiffel Tower again, everything
...bleeding into the horizon.

Cento III's lines consist of word clusters from Annabel Abbs' **The Joyce Girl,** *Sebastian Faulks'* **Paris Echo,** *Jeremy Mercer's* **Books, Baguettes and Bedbugs,** *Paula McLain's* **The Paris Wife** *and Edmund White's* **The Flâneur.**

Versailles — Spring, Winter

For decades your visit to the Château had been like a pearl clasped in your memory, taken out on rare occasions. How you'd slipped, like Goldilocks, into the Queen's Bed. The pull of embroidery on your skin, flip-flops adrift. How you'd planted a pouty pink kiss on the statue of Charlemagne, then twisted *like they did last summer* the length of the *Salon des Glaces*, backcombed high as Madame de Pompadour. How you'd hit the headlines chasing a sheep in the *hameau de la reine*. A sturdy little sheep *whose ancestors must surely have escaped the guillotine*.

Today, the Château squats, foreshortened, against a grey canvas. The Canal is heavy with ice. The statues and urns wear frost-proof shrouds. The winter sun blunts the edges of the garden. You lift your face. The pearl slips and slides like a pinball.

A postcard from the ex

It's been a long time, Paris   hope is the tail between my legs   it's
the not needing to explain   the sneaking back unnoticed   to prostrate
on the cobbles   grazed   marked   blessed   hope is the sparrow
pecking the rich dust between the roses in the Palais Royal   the
fearless cat at the wrong door   show me all your hidden tattoos,
Paris   I am ready to become your namesake

Paris is a paint-chart

the Seine is a porridgey *Drainpipe Grey*, the sky a blue called *Bardo*

the Ritz has repainted its walls with *Hemingway's Breath,* now the plaster whispers *I have liberated the wine cellars of Paris*

the Conciergerie has chosen *Sang de la Reine* for its banners and letterheads

even the dogshit is painterly, a *Brindled Roan*

the Parisians already speak of *le pandémie* and *le confinement* in the sepia tones of *la grippe espagnole*

my room is lit with a blurred off-white called *Nostalgie*, a colour where nothing can be the same

Paris is a paint-pot I have dipped my fingers in too often — the dripping red, white and blue unsure whether to be stripes or diagonals

what frauderie when home is a gentle palette of bluebell and samphire, the feathery grey of sea mist, the possibilities of rock salt; a place where lambs are knit tight into their new coats every spring

I rewild my face, chameleon country dweller, hot urban blood running through my veins in a neon I've never seen

Paris is a canvas for the street artists du monde and my bag is full of aerosols to scrimshaw my name on the bone-grey stone in all the shades of *mal du pays*

La Reine

I have lived before, in a château, under a mountainous wig, with skirts wide enough to hoard a lover; sliding sideways into gilt-edged rooms in slippy shoes to hide my hooves for I have lived before this before, eyes vulpine, hands scaled and clawed.

How I relish the stench of my havoc — powdered, teeth fashionably black, I am in thrall to poisons, love the bite of lead-white on my skin, love how hapless bones sculpt and cinch my waist, how a thousand tiny silkworms boil and unravel to cocoon my body.

Oh boredom, boredom, the fleas in my wig bloodying my scalp, endless flatterers, dirty hungry things crying at the gate, the rasp of sharpening knives.

Les Jardins du Ruisseau, Paris 18ème

I sit under the wisteria like an Impressionist heroine
brushed with French sunlight, a backdrop
of blushing valerian and dandelion-headed chives.
I crumble fallen flowers into a pot pourri
of violet and cream.

Gardens make me long for wide straw hats
that don't stay on, and bowls of strawberries
I don't really like.

Somewhere is the stream that gives the gardens their name.
We're all water diviners, a friend once said, but the sirens
of this busy city drown all watery hauntings.

I read the postcard I bought in the flea-market —
a sister's good wishes in hundred-year-old ink
to her brother, stationed in Verdun;
I think of all the things that could happen to my own brother
but don't.

The gardens grow along the platform
of an abandoned railway.
Maybe the postcard hurtled past this bench
into the hands of a soldier
who longed to discard
his mask of mud, scab, fleabite —
be blessed once more with Parisian dust.

I tell the bees I'm leaving —
it does not interrupt
their purposeful zig-zags across air
a blackbird briefly sings to gold.

In this garden I am Suzanne
who refuses to pronounce certain vowels,
was the best at French skipping,
wants a cat called Biscotte,
likes songs about oranges and madness.

The sky mumbles thunder —
it's time for the Métro's breathless embrace.
This afternoon I was the happy sovereign
of transitory things.

'the sovereign of transitory things' is a line from the writings of Robert de Montesquiou
(1855–1921)

Les Jardins du Ruisseau are community gardens in the 18ᵗʰ arrondissement along one of the
old platforms of the disused railway, La Petite Ceinture, which used to encircle Paris.

The Bees of Paris

there is news for her from the roof of Notre Dame
    how the hive vibrated their thousand thousand wings
to cool their Queen
    as fire turned buttery cells molten
how they started alarm-dance
    stripey gilets bristling
how the smoke came   lulled them
    how they woke to char and ruin
how a new Queen hatched to joy-dance
    how their honey tastes of wood-smoke and winter sunlight

if all the bees of Paris swarmed
    with their spoilt Queens
they would darken the city from Vincennes to Versailles
    but today they hum of forage in the window boxes of the 16ème
        lavender   violet   marigold
and in the Jardin du Luxembourg
    chestnut   lime acacia
the bees conjure a world of pollen-laden legs   tongues coarse with nectar

the bees believe the hives on the roof of the Opéra Garnier
    thrum and spill with liquid arias
cascading deep into damp and bony catacombs
    where a man ages honey wine
to make the streets sing of bliss and sting

Acknowledgements

In Which A Middle-Aged Woman in Primark Jeans Denies Her Invisibility was published in Poetry News (Autumn 2019). *I am building Paris in my bedroom* was published in Live Canon's 2021 International Poetry Competition Anthology. *Mon Cher Lucien* and *She is the woman I should have been* appeared in The French Literary Review (Spring 2022). *Bagatelle* and *Paris, C'est Une Blonde* were published in Revue [R]evolution and *Renée Vivien composes a ghazal for Violet Shillito* in Alchemy Spoon (Issue 6). *This City* (now called: *A reverse abecedarian in praise of Paris*) was highly commended in the Plough Poetry Prize (2022). *Zuihitsu: the year of the thief* appeared in Issue 28 of Long Poem Magazine. *Les Jardins du Ruisseau* was published in Spelt Magazine's Autumn 2022 Issue. *Où est le Métro s'il vous plait* and *Paris is a paint-chart* both appeared in *PISSOIR!* Autumn 2023. *Reincarnation as the Eiffel Tower* first appeared in the Beautiful Dragons anthology *Lighting Up* (2021). *Barbès Rochechouart, Versailles — Spring, Winter, In Printemps Department Store, This Place, This is Where, Flâneuse* and *Mapping It* all appeared in my début pamphlet, *Lumière* (Hedgehog Poetry Press 2018).

Hugest thanks, as always, to Heidi Williamson, my wonderful friend and mentor, whose gentle encouragement saw me through many iterations of this collection. Sally Walls, my dear, dear friend, your love of Paris keeps mine alive too, and many thanks for checking the use of French in the collection, any remaining errors are entirely at my door! *Paris Lit Up* at the *Culture Rapide* in Belleville and *Spoken Word Paris* are two warmly inclusive weekly open mic evenings where I aired many of these poems for the first time in situ. Jane Wilkinson, many thanks for all your inspiring ideas for the cover art.

Many thanks to Julia Webb and the Norwich Stanza for putting many of these poems through their paces, and Sarah Doyle's Sunday group whose enthusiasm and support was so energising during the never-ending aftermath of the pandemic.

The biggest thank-you of all goes to Chris, of course, for his endless patience and support as I uttered those immortal lines, "I think I need just one more trip to Paris…"

LIVE CANON